THE
CREEK
INDIANS

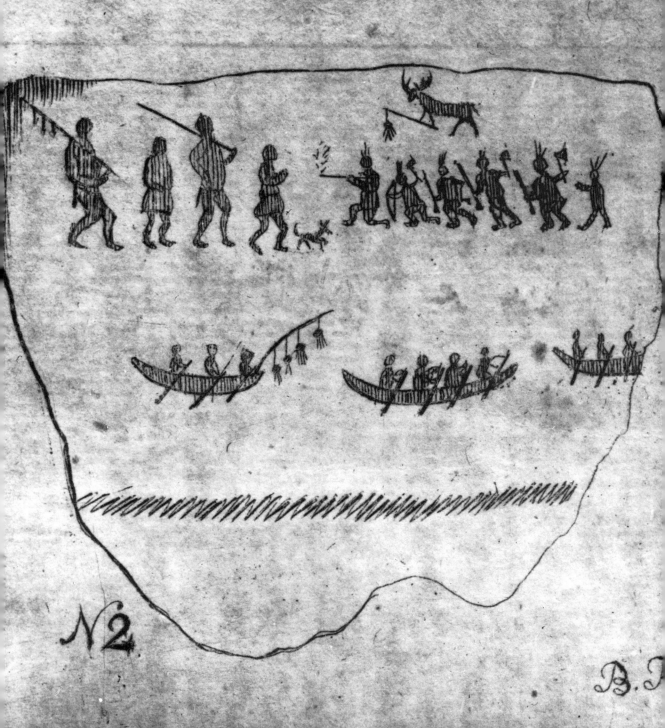

THE JUNIOR LIBRARY OF
AMERICAN INDIANS

THE CREEK INDIANS

Ellen Scordato

CHELSEA HOUSE PUBLISHERS
New York Philadelphia

FRONTISPIECE A line drawing made by a Creek war party, found in a place called Hoopah Ullah, or Noisy Owl

CHAPTER TITLE ORNAMENT Part of a beaded pouch that belonged to a Creek warrior

Chelsea House Publishers
EDITORIAL DIRECTOR Richard Rennert
EXECUTIVE MANAGING EDITOR Karyn Gullen Browne
EXECUTIVE EDITOR Sean Dolan
COPY CHIEF Philip Koslow
PICTURE EDITOR Adrian G. Allen
ART DIRECTOR Nora Wertz
MANUFACTURING DIRECTOR Gerald Levine
SYSTEMS MANAGER Lindsey Ottman
PRODUCTION COORDINATOR Marie Claire Cebrián-Ume

The Junior Library of American Indians
SENIOR EDITOR Sean Dolan

Staff for THE CREEK INDIANS
COPY EDITOR Margaret Dornfeld
EDITORIAL ASSISTANT Nicole Greenblatt
DESIGN ASSISTANT John Infantino
PICTURE RESEARCHERS Sandy Jones, Diana Gongora
COVER ILLUSTRATOR Vilma Ortiz

7 9 8 6

Library of Congress Cataloging-in-Publication Data

Scordato, Ellen.
The Creek Indians/by Ellen Scordato.
  p. cm.—(The Junior Library of American Indians)
Includes index.
Summary: Examines the life, culture, and future prospects of the Creek Indians.
        ISBN 0-7910-1660-9
        ISBN 0-7910-1974-8 (pbk.)
1. Creek Indians—Juvenile literature. [1. Creek Indians. 2. Indians of North America.] I. Title. II. Series.
E99.C9S36 1993   92-35972
973'.04973—dc20   CIP
                                                  AC

CONTENTS

A 20th-century artist's drawing of a Mississippian village. The Mississippians were the ancient ancestors of tribes like the Creeks and the Chickasaws.

CHAPTER **1**

Fire, a Lion, and War

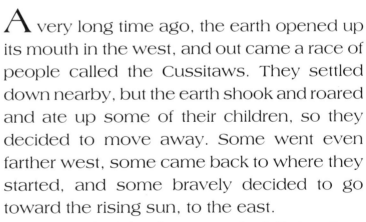

A very long time ago, the earth opened up its mouth in the west, and out came a race of people called the Cussitaws. They settled down nearby, but the earth shook and roared and ate up some of their children, so they decided to move away. Some went even farther west, some came back to where they started, and some bravely decided to go toward the rising sun, to the east.

Many colorful adventures befell the Cussitaws on the journey east, which would affect how they would live for hundreds of years. First they came to a thick, muddy river, where they rested overnight. Next morning, they traveled on and came to another strange river—this one was colored red. Here they fished and lived for two years. Still, they wanted to go farther. The Cussitaws followed the red river to its beginning, where they heard a loud noise like thunder and saw a mountain singing with the sound of a great fire from its top—a volcano. They took some of this fire for themselves and kept it burning.

Other kinds of fire came to them too. From the east came a white fire, which they did not like. From the south came a blue fire, and from the west came a black fire, and the people refused to use these, too. Finally, a red and yellow fire came from the north, and it pleased them. They mixed this with the mountain's fire and kept and used it forever.

Next they found four plants that sang to them and told the people how to use them for medicine. They also found a tall pole that restlessly bent and swayed and moaned in the wind. They made it quiet and took it to help them in battles.

Soon they met other people near the mountain—three other nations called the Chickasaws, the Alabamas, and the Abihkas. The four groups began to argue fiercely about who was the oldest, and they decided to have a contest to decide the question. Each nation set up a pole and tried to cover the pole with the scalps of their enemies. The Cussitaws quickly piled up so many that no one could even see their pole, and the Chickasaws and the Alabamas followed close behind. The Abihkas could not even pile up enough to reach their knees.

The Cussitaws continued to travel east, and they came to a town where the people had a terrible problem. Every seven days, a lion came rushing out of his cave and ate one of them. The Cussitaws promised to destroy the beast and help the people. First they dug a deep pit. Then they covered the pit with a net made of hickory bark and pile branches on top of the net. Quietly they crept up to the lion's den, then swiftly threw a noisy rattle into the cave. The angry lion rushed out and chased them through the woods. The Cussitaw hunters cleverly led him on a chase to the pit, which was hidden by the net and branches. The lion rushed over the net and fell into the deep pit, where the Cussitaws killed him with burning pine branches. They kept his bones for good luck charms during wartime and continued their journey.

The Cussitaws crossed rivers and creeks and came upon more towns filled with peo-

ple. When they did, they shot white arrows into the town. If the townspeople shot back white arrows, the Cussitaws treated them peacefully. But if the arrows came back red, the Cussitaws made war on the village. Finally they came to a town where the people called themselves Palachucolas. These people were friendly, offered the Cussitaws white feathers as a sign of friendship, and asked to live with them in harmony under

A traditional Creek village, painted by the modern-day Creek artist Larry McMurtry.

one chief. A river ran through the country there, and the Cussitaws divided into two groups. Some continued to call themselves Cussitaws and lived on one side of the river, whereas others called themselves Cowetas and lived on the other side. The story of how they discovered fire, medicine, and strength in war was passed down from grandparents to parents to children, over and over again.

These people, the Cussitaws and the Cowetas, formed part of the group of tribes that the early European settlers in North America called the Creek Indians. In 1737, an old Indian man named Cheilli told the story of the different-colored fires and the lion to a British general on the site of what would become the modern city of Savannah, Georgia. But when Chekilli told the story, Georgia did not exist as a state. In fact, the United States did not yet exist as an independent country, and at that time people from England, Spain, and France were just beginning to settle in large numbers in the south-eastern part of North America. The arrival of the European settlers had already greatly changed the way the Creeks lived, and more changes were in store. ▲

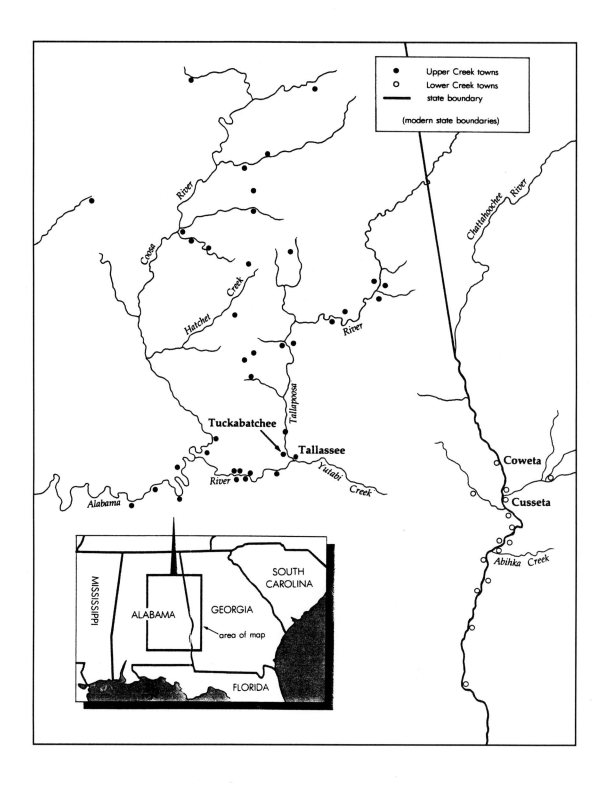

Upper Creek towns
Lower Creek towns
state boundary

(modern state boundaries)

Coosa River

Chattahoochee River

Hatchet Creek

River

Tallapoosa

Tuckabatchee

Tallassee

Yutabi Creek

River

Alabama

Coweta

Cusseta

Abihka Creek

MISSISSIPPI

ALABAMA

GEORGIA

SOUTH CAROLINA

area of map

FLORIDA

The villages of the Creek nation were spread out along rivers in eastern Alabama and western Georgia.

CHAPTER **2**

Arrival of the Newcomers

The Creek Indians who lived in what are now the states of Georgia and Alabama were not a closely knit nation when Europeans first began to settle North America in the 1600s. Instead, the Creeks were different, independent groups that formed friendships, or alliances, with each other. Most groups lived together in valleys near rivers, where the land was easy to farm and produced many crops. Their way of life was organized around providing food for themselves, and they did this in several ways.

Men and women each had their own duties and tasks to perform. Neither group was considered more important than the other. Women worked in the fields where the crops were

grown. Female family members worked together—mothers, sisters, grandmothers,
aunts, and cousins. They tilled the soil with
digging sticks and hoes fitted with points of
bone or sharpened stone. Corn (also called
maize), beans, and squash were among the
vegetables they grew. Women and children
also gathered nuts, berries, roots, and
herbs as well as special plants such as but-
ton snakeroot, ginseng, and red cedar, from
which the Creek made medicines.

Men caught fish in the rivers with spears
and bows and arrows. Sometimes they
stretched fences made of woven branches
across streams to trap fish. One of the most
unusual ways they caught fish was by
pounding special plant roots into powder and
sprinkling the water with it. The plant roots
contained a poison that stunned the fish and
made them float to the surface where they
could be gathered. The poison did not hurt
people who ate it. Men also hunted together
in the forests for deer, bears, rabbits, and
squirrels. Hunting was hard work, not a sport.
The community needed the meat for food
and used animal skins for clothes.

Creek communities were called *italwas*.
They reminded the British settlers and explorers of towns, and soon the English settlers called the Creek communities towns
rather than italwas. Each town was inhabited

by an independent group of people who did not consider themselves responsible to any other group. They had different histories and customs from other groups, but they also had many things about their way of life in common with these others. Two major divisions of Creek towns developed. The *Lower Towns* lined the Chattahooche and Flint rivers in what is now Georgia. The *Upper Towns* were 100 miles away, in what is now Alabama, along the Coosa, Tallapoosa, and Alabama rivers.

Every important Creek town had a large, rectangular, open space called the square ground. Around this were long, low buildings with no fronts that were filled with seats facing the square. During the summer, religious ceremonies took place in the square, and when visitors from other towns arrived, they were entertained there. Councils were held there in the summer, too, and in the winter councils were held in *chakofas*, tall, cone-shaped buildings where a special fire burned. Most Creeks lived in family compounds spreading out away from the square ground. The compounds had several buildings, gardens, and huge fields.

Each compound belonged to a family, and all the members of that family belonged to the same *clan*. Creek clan names included the Wind clan, the Bird clan, the Alligator clan,

and the Bear clan. They consisted of many more members than just a father, mother, and children. In fact, Creek families were organized very differently. Creek people traced their family tree only through their mother. Children were part of the mother's clan and were considered to be related to all her relatives, but not to their father's relatives. Girls learned the skills they needed from their mother, and boys learned from their mother's brothers, their uncles. The father was responsible for teaching his own sisters' boy children, his nephews.

A chief governed each town and took care of public matters such as receiving official visitors from other towns, storing the main food supply, and communicating with others on behalf of the town. A group of older, distinguished men formed a council that helped the chief and decided the right time for war and ceremonies.

The Creeks lived this way for hundreds of years, providing everything they needed for themselves and occasionally trading with other tribes. The arrival of Europeans from Spain, France, and England changed their

This drawing of the inside of a Creek family dwelling was done in the early 18th century.

way of life greatly. In the 17th century, the British founded their colony of Carolina and its capital of Charles Town in what was basically Creek territory. From Charles Town the British came, eager to trade with the Creeks. They wanted deerskins and captured Indians from other tribes to employ as slaves. They offered guns, ammunition, European clothing and cloth, metal tools and weapons, copper and tin pots and pans, and many other things. All this changed the way Creeks acted, for to get the guns, cloth, and metal, they had to concentrate on providing enough captured Indians and deerskins to pay for them.

Men went away for long periods of time to make war with other tribes and bring back prisoners. The Creeks were successful, skillful warriors and soon became the wealthiest Indians in the Southeast. Other, smaller Indian groups who were not as powerful or had fewer British guns were destroyed. One group, the Yamassees, were so enraged by the situation that in 1715 they attacked and killed several hundred British settlers—most of the British who lived outside the city of Charles Town. Two years later, in 1717, the British colonial government declared Indian slave trading illegal.

The Spanish and the French also traded with the Creeks. When the British tried to raise prices and charge too much for their goods, the Creeks could sometimes get better trading terms from the Spanish and French. Even so, all the Europeans wanted deerskins. In order to be able to buy European goods, the Creeks concentrated on deer hunting. Creek men killed so many deer in their own territory that soon they had to travel very far to find any more to kill. Women and old men stayed in the towns to raise the crops the Creeks needed, but soon they became so used to farming and sewing with metal hoes and needles bought from the Europeans that after a few generations, no one remembered how to live without such things.

At the same time that more and more British were coming to the Southeast, the Span-

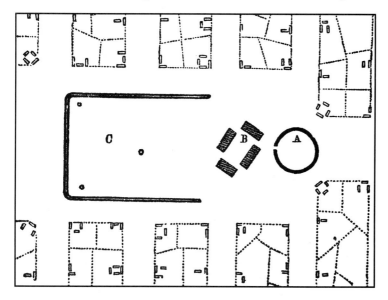

William Bartram, an early American scientist and explorer, made this chart of a typical Creek town in the 18th century. The letter A designates the tall, circular chakofa, or council house. The letter B designates the town square. The letter C designates a field used for sports and games. Family compounds surround the center of town.

ish claimed all of what is now the state of Florida. The French also wanted to control part of Florida and built new forts there, and all three groups wanted the Creeks to be on their side. The Creeks had a hard time deciding what to do, and not every town felt the same way. Finally, a large council was held, with chiefs from many towns. Brims, the chief of a town called Coweta, suggested they support not one but all three European powers. They would trade with all but not side with one against the others. Brims's idea made it possible for the Creeks to stay free and independent. All the towns agreed in 1720, and soon the independent Creeks were the most powerful nation in the Southeast.

By the middle of the 18th century, the struggle among the European powers for control of the eastern part of North America led to war. The French and Indian War ended in 1763 with complete victory for the British. England gained control of all the land France had in what is now Canada. The British also controlled the entire eastern coast of North America. The Creeks could no longer decide for themselves whom they wanted to deal with—they had to deal with the British alone. Independence and freedom became harder to keep, but the Creeks were powerful and determined. Soon, that would not be enough. ▲

CHAPTER 3

Independence for the Creeks?

After the French and Indian War, it seemed that every boat from England that came to the Southeast brought more settlers who wanted Creek land. In 1760, 6,000 whites and 3,500 black slaves lived in the British colony of Georgia, but by 1773, 18,000 whites and 15,000 black slaves lived there. Many of these white settlers thought they could take whatever land they wanted. Settlers did not believe the Creeks actually owned the land they lived on. Tension grew. The king of

England tried to solve this problem by appointing a superintendent of Indian affairs to settle arguments between Indians and colonists. Several men held this job, and they met often with the Creeks. The Creeks began to sell land that they considered worthless to the British, but that was not enough. Farmers and hunters took what they wanted, and the superintendent had a hard job. Because the superintendents tried to be fair the Creeks came to respect them, but they hated the colonists.

Soon, for many reasons, the colonists wanted to be free of British control, and in 1776, the American Revolution, or War of Independence, broke out. The Creeks refused to take sides, remembering that they had done well in the past by refusing to ally with the French, the Spanish, or the British. This time their strategy did not work as well. The colonists won the war, and the Creeks discovered that the British had surrendered control of America. What they could not understand was how suddenly their land was given to the new nation, the United States of America. How could one country give Creek land to another when the Creeks did not agree this arrangement? Instead of dealing with the British about trading and land, the Creeks now had to defend themselves against a country that threatened their very existence. The new government formed the states of Georgia and Alabama, and they included much Creek land.

One Creek leader, Alexander McGillivray, tried to convince the Creek towns to band together into one nation, so they could deal with the United States on more equal terms. He tried to make the *Creek National Council*, a group of leaders from Creek towns, into a powerful authority. But each Creek town was used to running its own affairs, and some Creek leaders resented McGillivray. They made treaties, or agreements, on their own and sold land. Many Creeks were not happy about the sales and refused to give up their land. The state of Georgia wanted to send soldiers to take the land by force, but its militia was not powerful enough. The Creeks, led by McGillivray, easily kept the Georgians out of Creek territory.

In 1787, representatives of every state came together to agree to the Constitution, which established a strong federal government for the United States. McGillivray quickly decided to deal with this new power. He and other leaders went to the capital and signed a treaty in which the United States recognized the independence of the Creeks and promised to protect the boundaries of the Creek nation. McGillivray then went back to the Creeks, hoping to convince the dif-

Benjamin Hawkins was the U.S. superintendent for Indian affairs in the southeast from 1796 to 1816. He was responsible for introducing many non-Indian ways to the Creeks.

ferent towns to band together into one strong nation, just as the states had banded together to form the United States. Before he could do so, he died at the age of 34. The Creeks were still without one central government.

Next, the United States tried to make the Creeks behave like the white U.S. citizens. Missionaries came to change their religious beliefs to Christianity. Superintendents of Indian affairs convinced some Creeks to establish farms owned by one family and worked by slaves and to sell their products in markets. Some Creeks, especially those in the Lower Towns in the east near Georgia, did change their way of life. Other Creeks, in the Upper Towns, were insulted and clung to their own ways. Tension between the two groups grew.

Open war broke out when one group of Creeks decided to follow the advice of Tecumseh, a war leader from the Shawnee Indians, who said Indians should band together and resist all non-Indian ways. A band of Creeks who visited him and agreed with his ideas was journeying back home when they met and murdered some white settlers The superintendent of Indian affairs, Benjamin Hawkins, asked that Creek lawmenders, or police, capture the murderers. Instead, they killed the accused Indians. A huge outcry arose among the Creeks, for it was terrible to them that one group of Creeks should murder another at the command of a non-Indian. In response, a group of prophets called the *Red Sticks* arose. The Red Sticks wanted all Creeks to return to traditional ways and stop behaving like whites by buying goods, selling their crops, living in non-Indian houses, and generally acting just like the non-Indian farmers. They wanted all whites and all Creeks who chose to live like whites to leave Creek land. They also fought Creek leaders who did not agree with them.

In 1813, the Red Stick prophets began to attack Creeks who had adopted white ways. They burned farms and killed cows and hogs belonging to Creeks who lived like non-In-

In the early part of the 19th century, the Shaw-nee leader Tecumseh tried to convince the In-dian tribes of the East to unite against American settlement. Tecumseh had a great influence on the Creeks.

dians. One Creek, Big Warrior, gathered those who did not agree with the Red Sticks into his fort, Tuckabatchee, for protection. Soon they were surrounded by Red Sticks. Hawkins sent a rescue mission to Tuckabatchee under the command of a Lower Towns Creek warrior named William McIntosh. He and his forces rescued the people in the fort and led them to safety in the Lower Towns.

By this time, the Creeks were deeply divided. Small battles often broke out between the two groups—the Red Sticks and their followers and those who supported white ways. After one such skirmish in which a group of Red Sticks were attacked, they mounted a bloody counterattack in revenge. In 1813, they attacked Fort Mims, a plantation in Alabama where 300 people lived. Some were white, a few were Creek, and most were from families that included both Creeks and whites. The Red Sticks were very successful warriors. In their well-planned attack they killed almost 260 people at Fort Mims, but the response was even more bloody.

Whites in the surrounding area were enraged. Until then, they thought the arguments among the Creeks did not affect them. Suddenly, they saw that they could also be victims. They not only wanted revenge but also

William McIntosh is one of the most controversial figures in Creek history. He and his followers sided with Andrew Jackson and his troops in the United States's war against the Creeks, and he later agreed to sell much Creek land to the U.S. government.

saw a chance to kill Indians and steal their land. Armies of white settlers from the states of Georgia, Tennessee, and Mississippi invaded Creek land. The largest group, from Tennessee, was led by General Andrew Jackson. The followers of William McIntosh helped them, and together they rampaged through Upper Creek areas, killed 3,000 Creeks, and finally defeated the forces of the Red Sticks and the traditional Creeks at the Battle of Horseshoe Bend.

The defeated Creeks were forced by Jackson to sign the Treaty of Fort Jackson. Without payment, they had to give up 25 million acres of Creek land in Alabama and Georgia. For the first time, Creek land had been invaded and taken by force. Fifty years earlier, in 1763, the Creeks had been confident that they could deal with non-Indians on their own terms. By 1814, they were divided and defeated, and their enemy was becoming stronger and more powerful every year. ◣

David B. Mitchell was named federal agent to the Creeks in 1816. He worked to take the Creeks' land from them and give it to the white settlers.

CHAPTER **4**

Struggle for the Homeland

The Treaty of Fort Jackson marked the first time that the Creeks had been defeated by their enemies. They had given up much of their land, and the areas in Georgia and Alabama that they had kept had been almost ruined by the 1813–14 war—soldiers had burned houses, barns, and fields and had killed livestock. Even worse, more settlers kept coming, and many of them wanted Creek land. In 1810, 9,000 non-Indians lived in Alabama; in 1820, 128,000 lived there. Most of the new settlers did not see why they could not simply take land where no one—but Indians—lived.

The Creeks struggled to keep the land they had, where they farmed and lived together, but the terms of the struggle had changed. They could no longer depend on their warriors to fight the non-Indians, and so they dealt with the non-Indians through treaties. But both dishonest non-Indians and greedy Creeks made this path a dangerous one.

The president of the United States at the time, James Madison, appointed a new federal agent named David B. Mitchell. Mitchell was determined to take all the Creek land for non-Indian settlers and had no interest in helping the Creeks. He did not hesitate to bribe, or secretly pay, certain Creek leaders to convince them to sell the land that belonged to the Creeks as a whole, even though most of the Creeks did not want to sell. One leader in particular, William McIntosh, worked closely with Mitchell for his own gain and his tribe's loss.

McIntosh was the son of a Creek mother and a Scottish father. He came from Coweta, the largest Creek town in the Lower Towns. Because he spoke English very well, government officials tended to want to do business with him. They misunderstood his position as a Lower Creek leader and thought he was

continued on page 41

TRADITIONAL FABRICS

Before the 16th century, Creek women made clothing, bags, and other objects for everyday and ceremonial use out of animal skins and plant fibers. When the European explorers began to travel through Creek territory, the Creeks were introduced to many new things, such as glass beads, wool, and cotton fabric. Eventually, the Creeks blended the Europeans' fabrics and decorating ideas with their own, and the result was a creative blend of Indian and European design.

Today, Creek women still make garments similar to those of their ancestors. Although this clothing is now worn only at ceremonies, it continues to show the unique heritage of the Creeks.

Two sashes woven from strands of dyed wool, about 26 inches long. The Creeks usually wore sashes only on ceremonial occasions.

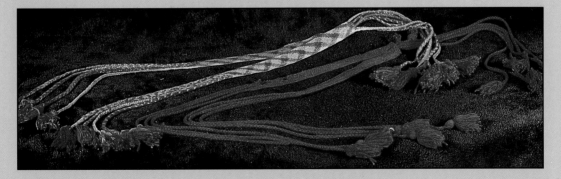

An early-18th-century pouch and belt woven on a loom from wool yarn. The edge of the flap is decorated with white glass trade beads. The item was owned by Creek leader and prophet Josiah Francis.

A mid-19th-century pouch and belt made from several pieces of dyed red strouding—a coarse wool manufactured by the British for trade with the Indians. The items are embellished with glass trade beads and yarn tassels.

Creek women made some types of clothing and other objects using a special technique known as finger weaving. By hand, finger weavers braided multiple strands of yarn, sometimes with beads attached, to create bands of fabric. They often left the ends unbraided to form tassels. The process was much cheaper and faster than weaving on a loom, but it also had limitations. Finger weavers could manage just a few strands of yarn at a time, so they could only produce garments that could be made from narrow fabric strips, such as sashes, garters, and other types of clothing.

A mid-20th-century man's sash that was worn during ceremonial games played between teams representing different Creek towns.

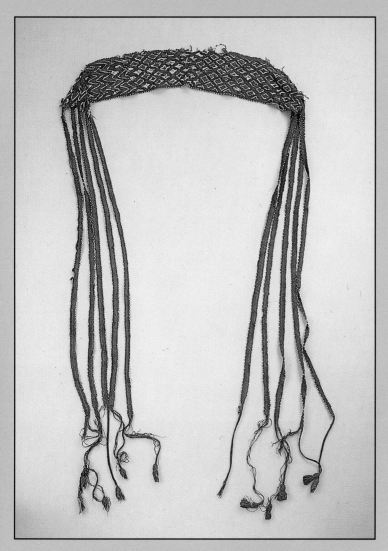

A ceremonial belt, approximately six feet long, made of yarn interwoven with white porcelain beads.

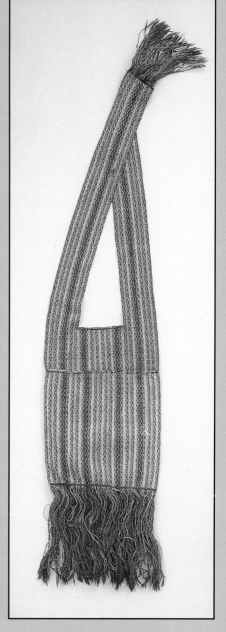

A late-18th-century pouch and belt made with European yarn and glass beads.

The breechcloth was one of the most common articles of clothing worn by Indian men and women. The garment, which consisted of a center piece and two flaps, was worn between the legs and held in place around the waist by folding the flaps over a belt.

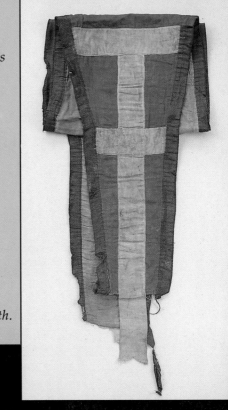

An early-20th-century cotton breechcloth.

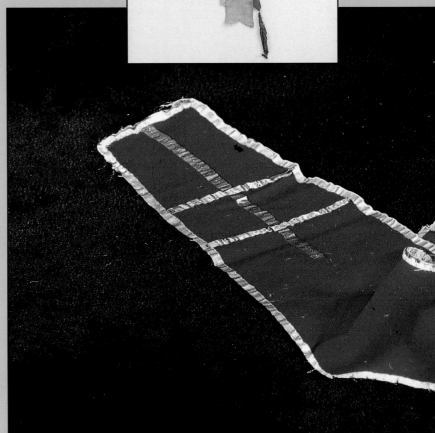

A flannel breechcloth from the 1890s, decorated with satin ribbon appliqué.

The four white crosses on this breechcloth, made in 1964, represent four allied Creek towns. The black central cross symbolizes the four corners of the world.

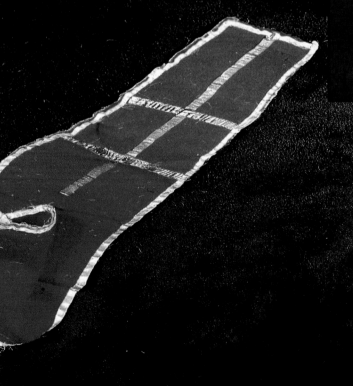

*A Creek man's ceremonial sash, approximately 55 inches long, made in 1964
as part of his ceremonial game garb.*

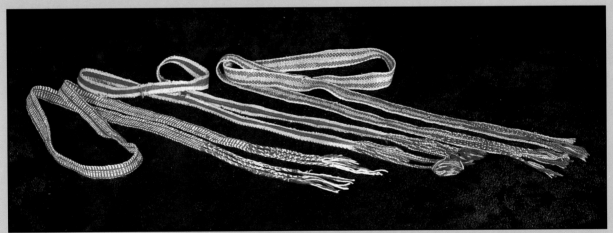

Three early-20th-century fringed sashes.

continued from page 32

the sole representative of the Lower Creeks. McIntosh did not tell them otherwise.

Pressure on the Creeks to sell their land and leave the area increased. In 1802, the federal government had agreed to help the state of Georgia obtain all Indian land within its borders—both the Creek land in the east and the Cherokee land in the north. The agreement also said the Indians did have the right to refuse to sell, and they exercised that right, firmly refusing all offers. But in 1812, U.S. government officials managed to bribe McIntosh and several leaders into selling half the Creeks' land in Georgia. McIntosh received almost $40,000 and several valuable pieces of land for his own use. The Creeks' situation became more desperate. They had to do something to stop McIntosh and others from selling their land out from under them.

The Creek National Council still existed, but it was not strong. Decisions made by the council could not be enforced—the towns and individual leaders voluntarily agreed to do what the Council said. That finally changed. Six years after McIntosh's first land sale, the Council drew up a written code of laws that stated that all land within Creek borders was nationally owned and could not be sold without the Council's approval. The penalty for disobedience was death.

The Council did not actually execute any-
one for breaking this law right away, but they
made sure all the leaders knew of the decree.
At the same time, Georgia and the United
States remained determined to get all the
Creek land. On December 7, 1824, a group of
U.S. treaty commissioners opened talks with
the Creek leaders at a town called Broken
Arrow. The president told the commissioners
to buy all the Creek land and promise the
Indians they would receive land in the West,
which had not been divided into states yet.
The government also said it would pay for
the Creeks' moving expenses.

The Creek leaders refused the offer. One
speaker, Opothle Yoholo, said he "would not
take a house full of money" for Creek land.

But afterward, McIntosh invited the commissioners to his tavern at Indian Springs and
said he would sell them all the lands in Georgia and Alabama if they paid him enough,
even though he knew he was breaking Creek
law. The commissioners told the president of
the offer, but he refused to sign an agreement
with only one self-appointed Creek leader,
recognizing the wrongness of such a treaty.
The commissioners went ahead and signed
the Treaty of Indian Springs with McIntosh.
McIntosh and a few hundred of his asso-
ciates and relatives got $200,000 and extra

The Creek leader Opo-thle Yoholo vowed that he "would not take a house full of money" for Creek land, but later he helped negotiate the Treaty of Washington.

money for land they did actually own. Opo-thle Yoholo was present when the treaty was signed and warned McIntosh of the danger he had put himself in by his dishonest action.

The Creek National Council was aghast. Quickly they took action and pronounced the death sentence on McIntosh, two of his sons-in-law, and an associate. On April 29, 1825, 200 Creek lawmenders went to McIntosh's home and arrested the 4 condemned men. They were executed the next day.

The Georgia authorities were angry, for the Creeks obviously refused to accept the Treaty of Indian Springs. The Creeks went even further, and after months of appeals to Washington they managed to get the United States to declare the treaty null and void. Never before and never again did the United States agree to tear up a treaty, no matter how fraudulent or illegal. The new Treaty of Washington, negotiated by Opothle Yoholo and others, stated that the Creeks would sell all their land in Georgia but keep their land in Alabama. They received $250,000 plus $20,000 per year forever for the nation. Also, the treaty allowed the followers and descendants of William McIntosh to emigrate to land marked for them in the area west of the Mississippi River. Large numbers of Creeks did remove themselves from the East, but a great many decided to stay. In fact, immense disagreement arose among different Creek groups over the issue of moving west.

At the same time, there were many disagreements among non-Indians about whether all the Indians should be removed from the East. Some argued that passing a law to force all eastern Indians to leave their homeland and move west of the Mississippi was immoral and betrayed all the treaties that had been signed with the Indians. Others, including Andrew Jackson, who became president in 1828, argued that there was not enough room for both Indians and U.S. citizens and their slaves in the Southeast and that the Indians had to be forced out for the good of all. Jackson and his supporters won the argument in Congress. In 1830, the *Indian Removal Act* was passed, signed by Jackson, and became U.S. law.

Supposedly, the five most powerful and populous southeastern Indian tribes—the Creeks, Choctaws, Cherokees, Chickasaws, and Seminoles—would be paid for the loss of their land and homes, have all their travel and moving expenses paid for by the government, and legally receive property in the West. According to the Removal Act, they would not have to move unless they agreed to do so.

In practice, things were different. The Choctaws, Seminoles, and Chickasaws were forced to sign treaties of removal. The Creeks signed a different treaty that allowed them to stay if they agreed to own plots of land in Alabama as individuals instead of keeping land as a nation. In return, the governments

of Alabama and the United States would keep intruders out of the little bit of land left to the Creeks.

The state of Alabama and the U.S. government did not hold up their end of the treaty. Through the next six years, non-Indians entered Creek territory, staked claims to land, and harassed the Indians who lived there. No one protected the Creeks. Alabama decided the Creeks were not citizens and so could not defend themselves in court. Non-Indians began to claim that Creeks owed them money, and when Creeks could not disprove these charges, they lost their land in payment for these imaginary debts. The Creeks' frustration mounted.

Finally, the situation turned into a tragedy. When a group of Georgians came to Alabama to join in stealing Creek land, a band of Creeks attacked them, then burned a steam-

In the winter of 1836-37, the Creeks were forced to leave their homeland and move to the Indian Territory across the Mississippi River. Nearly 40 percent of the Creek tribe died on the move west. The 20th-century Creek artist Jerome Tiger painted this picture of the tragic Creek exodus.

boat and a bridge. Jackson seized on the violence as an excuse to attack the Creeks with all the power of the U.S. Army. He ordered all Creeks to be rounded up and sent west.

The removal took place in the winter of 1836–37—during the worst of the winter. The Creeks were herded together like beasts. Only the very old, infants, and children rode in rickety wagons; the rest had to march on foot, and few had enough warm clothing or food. They were marched west for miles through cold mud and over frozen ground. Those who died on the way were left on the side of the road, where their bodies rotted or were eaten by wild animals. The few hundred who were lucky enough to be shipped up the Mississippi were packed onto unsafe, overcrowded steamboats. One of the boats, run by drunken crewmen, sailed up the wrong side of the river and crashed into another boat. Half the Creeks drowned when the boat sank after the collision. The rest were scalded by the exploding steam engine.

All the treaties the Creeks had signed were in vain. By 1840, the Creek nation ceased to exist in the East. Their homeland was gone forever. ▲

A Creek woman and child in the Indian territory.

CHAPTER **5**

A New Land, a New Nation

When the eastern Creeks reached Indian Territory in 1837, they encountered the followers of William McIntosh who had begun to settle there 10 years earlier. William's half brother, Roley McIntosh, was their leader. They had struggled to remake their lives in the West and had established homes, farms, and their own small, independent Creek republic. As in the East, these Creeks embraced the ways of their non-Indian neighbors, growing corn and cotton and owning slaves.

To avoid conflict between the eastern Creeks and the western Creeks, most of the eastern Creeks arranged to settle on the southwestern part of the Creek land in the West, along the Canadian River. Some settled with the western Creeks. In time, the division between newcomers and old settlers, and between Upper Town and Lower Town Creeks, blurred and changed. The major division developed between those who embraced non-Indian ways and lived near the Arkansas River and those who preferred traditional ways, such as owning land in common, and lived near the Canadian River. About 50 miles divided the two main settlements.

The Creeks' new homeland in the Indian Territory was in the eastern portion of what would become the state of Oklahoma.

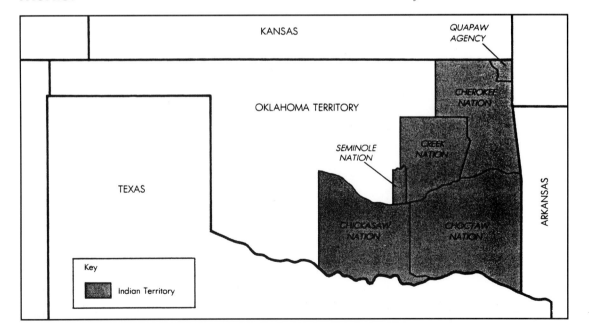

The two groups formed a new National Council in 1840. Meetings were held in a large council house built halfway between the two settlements, and each settlement elected its own principal chief. Roley McIntosh represented the Arkansas Creeks; a variety of leaders held the office for the Canadian Creeks, but Opothle Yoholo remained the most influential member of that group.

The council worked until 1859 or 1860, when a new written constitution reorganized the government. The new system did not take effect immediately, however. The year 1860 marked the beginning of the bloody Civil War, which ripped apart the United States. The Union states of the North battled the southern states of the Confederacy to keep them from breaking away from the United States, in part over the issue of slavery. The North wanted slavery to be illegal; the South supported slavery, for its entire society and economy was based on it.

The Creeks once again faced a difficult choice—which side should they support? When the southern states seceded (declared independence) in 1860–61, the Creek nation had to decide what to do. Because many Creeks owned slaves and had been to college in the South, they supported the Confederacy. This group, including Chilly and

Daniel McIntosh, signed a treaty of alliance with the Confederacy in 1861.

Opothle Yoholo and others, such as Oktarharsars Harjo (known to whites as Sands), also owned slaves but refused to ally with either side, claiming that taking sides in the white men's war could only hurt the independent Creeks. While the number of Confederate troops in Creek territory grew, Opothle Yoholo gathered those who wished to remain neutral at his plantation and then led his group north to the state of Kansas. Several thousand people traveled to Kansas with him. Harassed and attacked by Confederate troops on the way, they lost the wagons, livestock, and possessions they brought with them on the long, hard journey and arrived in Kansas poor and hungry. Although the Union army gave them tents to live in, Opothle Yoholo, who was nearly 80 years old, died from exposure while there.

The battles of the Civil War devastated Creek territory. Many Creeks fled to the Confederate South. By the time the Civil War ended in 1865, there was nothing left of the homes, farms, and livestock the Creeks had owned. All that was left was the land and the people, divided once again.

Two huge jobs faced both Creek groups—reestablishing the Creek nation and reopen-

The Creek leader Oktar-harsars Harjo, or Sands, advised his people to remain neutral during the Civil War and later opposed the establishment of a constitutional government for the Creeks. Sands was a traditionalist who regarded the new constitution as "the white man's law."

ing their relationship with the United States. Sands had become the leader of the Loyalists, or those who did not side with the Confederacy. Daniel McIntosh led the former Confederate allies. Both groups believed the United States would recognize their group as the right one to take control of the new Creek national government.

But the U.S. negotiators insisted on treating all Creeks like conquered enemies. They met in Washington, D.C., in January 1866 and forced the Indians to agree to a large land sale. They paid only $100,000 to the Loyalist Creeks for the property they lost during the war.

Through 1867, representatives of both Creek groups worked to create a new consti-

Samuel Checote won the first election for principal chief of the Creeks in 1867.

tution for the Creek nation. The one they finally agreed upon resembled that of the U.S. government, with a principal chief elected by adult male citizens, an elected legislature made up of two parts, the House of Kings and the House of Warriors, and a judicial branch with courts and judges. The first election for principal chief was held in November 1867 and was won by Samuel Checote, a Creek Methodist minister and former Confederate army officer. Sands was his opponent and remained so even after the election.

Although the constitution helped heal the differences between Confederate and Loyalist Creeks, it did not resolve the division between traditionalists and those embracing non-Indian ways. The groups' membership shifted and changed, but the division remained strong. Many traditional Creeks preferred the old National Council, made up of representatives of towns. They resented the new constitution, which Sands called "the same as the white man's law." These Creeks lived in traditional towns, kept their communal fields, were not Christians, and spoke their own Muskogee language rather than English. The other group called them "ignorant" for not preferring to live like non-Indians. Tensions mounted.

For years, Sands and his followers denounced the new Creek government and refused to pay attention to its decisions and decrees. In October 1871, 300 armed traditionalists broke up the annual National Council meeting. In 1875, Lochar Harjo, an important supporter of Sands (who died in 1872), was elected principal chief, but Checote's followers in the legislature removed him from office. Checote was reelected in 1879.

Finally, the situation came to a head in 1881. When Creek police broke up a meeting

Samuel Checote and some of his family sit in front of their home, a typical Creek dwelling in the Indian Territory.

of anti-constitution Creeks, violence broke out and the law officers were murdered. Checote called out the Creek militia, which chased several hundred anticonstitutionalists onto a nearby Kiowa *reservation*, where U.S. troops captured them and returned them to Creek territory. Checote made sure they knew they had lost the battle over the constitution. The traditionalists had been defeated, and the Creek nation went forward into the future armed with its new constitution. However, powerful forces were once more gathering to destroy the Creek nation. ▲

A Creek woman pounds corn into meal in the 1880s in the Indian Territory.

CHAPTER **6**

Facing the Future

The new threat to the Creek nation came from a new kind of invasion—cattlemen and ranchers drove their cattle through the nation on the way to market, railroad construction workers built tracks right through Creek land, and white intruders eagerly flocked to claim Creek land. The U.S. government encouraged these invaders, for a growing determination was building to make the Indians enter white society and stop living communally in their own nations.

In the 1880s, a group of federal officials wanted to reform the U.S. government's dealings with Indians. They believed the best way of life for the Indians was conforming to the way white Americans lived. To these reformers, forcing the Indians to give up everything that provided them a separate identity—their tribal government, their language, their religion, and their common ownership of land—was a way of helping them. Also, the Indians who lived on reservations in the Far West often suffered greatly when corrupt government employees stole their allotted food and supplies. Reformers saw the suffering of reservation Indians and grew more determined to change the Indian way of life entirely.

Unsurprisingly, the Creeks and the other four tribes who formed republics in Indian territory loudly opposed such measures. Despite their protests, Senator Henry Dawes proposed a bill that would force all Indians to divide communal land into small parts called *allotments* and assign them to individual tribespeople. The Dawes bill also abolished tribal governments and provided that communal land not used up in the allotment process would be sold. The bill became law in 1887 and is known as the General Allotment Act, or Dawes Act.

The Five Tribes in Indian territory were not covered by the act, but in 1893, Congress

Chitto Harjo, or Crazy Snake (standing at far right), and his followers were traditionalists who opposed the government's allotment plan. This picture was taken in 1901, after U.S. troops had arrested many of the Snake Indians, as Chitto Harjo's followers were known.

appointed Dawes as the head of a special commission to negotiate the law's application to the Creeks and others. The Creeks were horrified at the idea of allotment. When their representatives met the Dawes Commission, they rejected the proposals, as did the Choctaws, Chickasaws, Seminoles, and Cherokees. It made no difference. The Curtis Act of 1898 enforced allotment, abolished tribal courts, and required all laws passed by the tribal governments to be approved by the president of the United States. When the Creeks planned to sue the U.S. government

for violating the treaty of 1866, the president would not approve the act the Creek government passed to pay for the legal action.

Many Creeks then accepted allotment. Others totally rejected the allotment process. This group organized a resistance movement in the winter of 1900–1901. Their spokesman was Chitto Harjo, whose name meant "recklessly brave snake." Whites called him Crazy Snake, and all who organized to reject allotment were called Snake Indians. Chitto Harjo and the so-called Snake Indians set up a traditional Creek government at Hickory Ground, a town on the Canadian River, and passed laws banning allotment. In the spring of 1901, U.S. troops raided Hickory Ground and arrested 100 Creeks. They were brought to trial and threatened with hard prison terms unless they accepted allotment. Many promised to but did not, and in the end, only 1,331 Creek people accepted allotments—about 10 percent of those entitled to them.

Once allotment was over, another crisis loomed. Whites in Oklahoma Territory, just to the west of Indian Territory, wanted to become a state, and the Congress planned to combine the two areas in the state of Oklahoma. The five tribes of Indian Territory were appalled and tried to form their own

This picture of the Creek council house in Okmulgee was taken in 1905. Today, Okmulgee is home to a modern tribal center.

Indian state, to be called Sequoyah, after a respected Cherokee who had worked out a way to write the Cherokee language 80 years earlier. Members of the Five Tribes wrote a new state constitution, voted on it, passed it, and sent it to the U.S. Congress. Congress ignored it entirely, and in 1907 the state of Oklahoma joined the Union.

Through the beginning of the 20th century, many Creeks lived fairly well on their allotments. Still, serious troubles with the system existed. One problem arose because Indians were not allowed to sell their allotted land. This protection worked fine until, for instance, six Creek children inherited one allotment. Each of the six could not live on a small part of one allotment, but they could not buy more land, either. When the Creeks forced the government to remove the restriction on selling land, dishonest whites rushed in to swindle and cheat the Indians, many of whom were not used to the idea of owning land and did not understand taxes or real estate law. Some lost their land and lived in terrible poverty.

In the early 1900s, oil was discovered underground near the old Creek town of Tulsa, Oklahoma. Those families who lived on the allotments where oil was found then leased, or rented, their land to oil companies and received thousands of dollars a month in payment. Those who needed help dealing with such wealth, such as non-English-speaking Indians and orphans, were assigned guardians to take over the management of their allotments. These guardians did not hesitate to steal all the profits. One family of three orphans was discovered living in a hollow tree and scavenging for food by a state worker. The worker learned that the children owned allotments producing much oil—and money. Their guardian was stealing it all, lying about how he provided for the 3 orphans—as well as 51 other children for whom he was the guardian.

By the 1930s such abuses had helped reformers such as John Collier, the U.S. superintendent of Indian affairs, make a case for changing the allotment policy. The Indian Reorganization Act of 1934 and the Oklahoma Indian Welfare Act (OIWA) stopped allotment, established tribal or constitutional government for tribes, and provided federal funds to help Indians buy land to be held by tribes as a whole or to meet other needs in the Creek community.

The Creeks had done better than any other tribe in Oklahoma under allotment. Many families escaped swindlers and held onto their land, and some forms of town government remained. They were well equipped to take advantage of the OIWA. By supporting tribal incorporation and constitutions, the OIWA allowed the Creeks to re-create some of their national institutions. Although town govern-

Claude Cox has served as principal chief of the Creek nation for more than 20 years. During that time, the Creek economy has undergone a significant revival.

ment sometimes prevented the Creeks from focusing on affairs of the Creek nation as a whole, this situation gradually changed. When Congress finally allowed the Creeks to elect their own principal chief in 1971, they elected Claude Cox, a strong leader.

Cox has held office for 20 years. He presided over the construction of a national Creek complex of tribal offices in the capital of Okmulgee and fought for increased federal health care services, as well as for educational and employment programs and the construction of low-cost housing and various

The culture of the Creeks today is a blend of the traditional and the modern. Here, Creek women prepare to take part in a traditional stomp dance in Eufaula, Oklahoma. They are wearing rattles made of turtle shells and tin cans around their legs.

agricultural businesses. Today, the Creeks in eastern Oklahoma live on farms and in cities and towns, much like their non-Indian neighbors. There is no Creek reservation; the only tribally owned land is reserved for the capital complex, various businesses, and housing and health care centers. The Creeks do have their own special history, however, along with their tribal government, and they are justifiably proud of both.

Traditional ceremonies are still held each summer for those Creeks who choose to take part. Towns are still important in the lives of many Creeks and provide an important source of social and cultural identity. Town and ceremonial functions help link the Creeks of today with their ancestors, the Creeks of the distant past who first saw Europeans come to their homeland in southeastern America, and to those even farther back in time, the Cussitaws who climbed out of the mouth of the ground in the creation story and began their journey through time and space. ▲

CHRONOLOGY

ca. 1600s British found colony of Carolina and its capital Charles Town in Creek territory; Creeks begin to trade with the British, French, and Spanish

1763 French and Indian War ends, leaving the British in control of Creek territory

1783 American Revolution ends, leaving the United States in control of Creek territory

1813 Redstick prophets, who believe the Creeks should only follow traditional Indian ways, begin attacking Creeks who follow non-Indian ways

1814 Creeks are defeated by whites at Battle of Horseshoe Bend; the Indians sign Treaty of Fort Jackson, giving up 25 million acres of Creek land to the U.S. government

1824 Self-appointed Creek leader William McIntosh signs Treaty of Indian Springs, selling all the Indians' land in Georgia and Alabama to the U.S. government against the wishes of the Creek National Council

1825 U.S. government voids the Treaty of Indian Springs

1836–37 Creeks are forced to move West by U.S. government

1867 Creeks create new constitution resembling that of the U.S. government

1900 Creeks organize resistance movement against U.S. government's allotment policy

1971 U.S. government grants Creeks permission to elect a principal chief

GLOSSARY

allotment   U.S. government policy of the late 1800s that sought to divide land owned by a tribe into small tracts owned by individuals; also, one of these tracts

chakofas   tall, cone-shaped buildings where Creeks would gather for Winter Councils

clans   groups of Creeks that belonged to the same extended family and lived in the same compound

Creek National Council   a group of Creek town leaders that met to discuss the Indians' problems and decide policy

Italwas   Creek communities, which the British settlers and explorers called towns

Lower Towns   one of the two major divisions of Creek towns; they were located in Georgia

Redsticks   a group of Creek prophets that believed all Indian tribes should band together and resist non-Indian ways

removal   U.S. government policy of the early 1800s that forced the Indians in the eastern and southern United States to sell their land and move onto land west of the Mississippi River

reservation   an area of land set aside for use by Indians

Upper Towns   one of the two major divisions of Creek towns; they were located in Alabama

INDEX

ABOUT THE AUTHOR

Ellen Scordato is the copy manager at an advertising agency in New York City and a freelance writer and editor. She is the author of *Sarah Winnemucca* in Chelsea House's NORTH AMERICAN INDIANS OF ACHIEVEMENT series. She graduated magna cum laude from Wellesley College with a B.A. in classical civilization.

PICTURE CREDITS

DATE			